Scalping Stocks and Futures

Making Money with Top 5 Strategies

Andrew C. Ellis

© Copyright 2017 - All rights reserved.

In no way is it legal to reproduce, duplicate, or transmit any part of this document in either electronic means or in printed format. Recording of this publication is strictly prohibited and any storage of this document is not allowed unless with written permission from the publisher. All rights reserved.

The information provided herein is stated to be truthful and consistent, in that any liability, in terms of inattention or otherwise, by any usage or abuse of any policies, processes, or directions contained within is the solitary and utter responsibility of the recipient reader. Under no circumstances will any legal responsibility or blame be held against the publisher for any reparation, damages, or monetary loss due to the information herein, either directly or indirectly.

Respective authors own all copyrights not held by the publisher.

Legal Notice:

This book is copyright protected. This is only for personal use. You cannot amend, distribute, sell, use, quote or paraphrase any part or the content within this book without the consent of the author or copyright owner. Legal action will be pursued if this is breached.

Disclaimer Notice:

Please note the information contained within this document is for educational and entertainment purposes only. Every attempt has been made to provide accurate, up to date and reliable complete information. No warranties of any kind are expressed or implied. Readers acknowledge that the author is not engaging in the rendering of legal, financial, medical or professional advice.

By reading this document, the reader agrees that under no circumstances are we responsible for any losses, direct or indirect, which are incurred as a result of the use of information contained within this document, including, but not limited to, —errors, omissions, or inaccuracies.

TABLE OF CONTENTS

Intro

Tools For Scalping Successfully 1

Why Scalping Works 12

Scalping Stocks 17

Scalping Futures 27

Scalping on Currency Markets 38

Closing

INTRO

Scalping is a time-tested strategy that day traders use to make money in times that other strategies offer little opportunity for profit. This makes it attractive to traders in many markets, with many different styles, but it isn't for everyone. In order to be a successful scalper, you'll need a high tolerance for risk and fast reflexes that will allow you to enter and exit positions very quickly. The margins for error are low on scalp trades.

If you're set on incorporating scalping strategies into your overall trading technique, there are some things you'll need to make sure you have before getting started. These prerequisites are key to setting yourself up for success as a scalper.

- A method of recordkeeping that you are comfortable with. Especially in the beginning, you'll need to backtest your outcomes against the eventual realities of the market in order to determine what's working for you and what isn't. Keep careful track of your entry and exit points, what pivot point and range calculators you used, and how much you made off of each trade. At the end of the day, compare your predictions against the movements of the market that actually occurred.

- A full day to devote to trading. If you only have an hour or two to spend during the day trading, scalping isn't likely to be successful for you. Most scalpers make dozens, if not hundreds, of small trades per day. If you make too few trades, you forfeit the inherent protection from risk that scalping provides.

- The ability to keep a cool head. If you tend to get nervous when you have to trade on the fly, scalping is going to be rough on your nerves. If you're great under pressure, though, this might be a great fit.

- If you do have the personality, resources, and desire to make scalping part of your career, you still need tools and specific strategies. That's where this book comes in. In the coming chapters, you'll find the knowledge you need to make the high-speed calls and detailed tactics to give you the edge.

TOOLS FOR SCALPING SUCCESSFULLY

As you'll see, no indicator alone is strong enough to base your entire strategy on. The only exception to this might be the price action itself, but even then, an additional indicator is a nice way to confirm what you believe the price action is telling you. Because of this, you'll need to find a way to combine the tools in this chapter in a way that you can use comfortably and that suits your needs as a trader. Not only will this make your life easier, it will make you a more successful trader. Because everyone out there is looking to make as much money as possible based on the exact same numbers, the more you can factor your personality and instinct into your trading plan, the more unique it will be. This is what will set you apart from the pack, so make sure you consider who you are as a person and a trader as you lay your plans.

Start by taking a look at the methods that the chartmakers use. If the methodology seems sound to you, try using them every day for a week or so. Incorporate them into your paper trades initially. If you are able to get comfortable with them quickly, great! If not, move onto another indicator. These are tools you'll be using incredibly often; you want to be comfortable with them.

You'll also need to match the charts and indicators you use to the type of scalping you're doing. Obviously, the market you choose to trade on should be reflected, but also take into account the size of your trades and how many you plan on making per day. Different oscillators and indicators will be more suited to your plan than others. It's worth your time to find them.

You'll also want to make sure the charts you're using mesh well with the interface your broker offers. If their site reflects Bollinger bands on the main trading page, for instance, you probably will want to become familiar with how to read them. If you're going to be trading in index funds, you'll want to have a chart that reflects index volatility, and so on. Make sure your charts, your broker, and your trading goals are all well aligned.

1 and 5 Minute Candlesticks

Candlestick charts are the most fundamental information sources available to traders, but they are avoided by many. The reason for this is simple: they just don't feel comfortable reading them. There are many sites and pundits that will happily interpret the candlestick data into more familiar forms, but as a day trader, you don't have the luxury of waiting for them to translate for you. You'll absolutely have to get used to reading candles and reading them accurately.

These charts mean the same things on shorter timeframes as they do for the daily price action. The 1 and 5 minute candlestick charts simply slice the data more finely, giving the changes in, obviously, one or five minutes. These charts are invaluable because they're the clearest way to read price action. They do have weaknesses, though. Chiefly, they are susceptible to a time lag. You can make up for this weakness by using other charts that give more weight to the most recent data.

EMA

The exponential moving average, or EMA, is a perfect compliment to the price action from candlestick charts. It is calculated to give the most weight to the most recent price moves, so it's a more accurate reflection of what is coming. For day traders, the 12-day EMA is the most applicable. Its main utility to a scalper is to warn of upcoming breakouts or large momentum shifts. Since the majority of scalping takes place in a range-bound market, it's important to be able to pinpoint price areas where the range is likely to be broken.

MACD

The Moving Average Convergence Divergence is a chart that combines exponential moving averages in order to identify overbought or underbought securities. Alone, the MACD is not fine-tuned enough to be useful to a day trader, but it can confirm suspicions about market trends. A "signal line" is plotted on this chart as well as the MACD line, and it is the relationship between these two that you'll need to read. Broadly, when the two lines diverge, it is a signal that the current trend is coming to an end. When the lines cross over one another, it gives a clue as to whether the upcoming trend is bearish or bullish. If the MACD crosses the signal line from below, ending up above the signal, it is a bullish indicator. Conversely, when the MACD drops below the signal line, it's a bearish indicator.

RSI

The relative strength index, or RSI, is a momentum indicator that is very useful in identifying whether a security is over- or underbought. RSI values range from 0 to 100, with values above 70 indicating a security that has been overbought and values below 30 indicating that the security is somewhat underbought. In both these cases, the price is likely to correct itself, which means a trend reversal.

Watching for points where the RSI and the price action diverge is particularly useful in predicting whether a strong trend change is upcoming. When the price drops but the RSI does not, it is a bullish signal, and vice versa. If you have reason to suspect an end to a current range and need to estimate the direction a breakout will take, for instance, the RSI can be very useful.

Level II Quotes

Level II quotes are orders for stocks traded on the Nasdaq. They are ranked by best bid and ask prices from each market maker or participant in the market. These can give you a deeper insight into what is driving the price action, which lets you know how stable (or unstable) the price action is. Market makers can cloak their actions by buying smaller lots or timing their buys to string out other bidders, so take what you learn on level II quotes with a grain of salt. Where this information is really useful to a day trader is in quickly gauging the liquidity of a security or other asset. High numbers of orders translate into greater liquidity, which then translates into greater volatility. Depending on the market you're in and what your strategy indicates, high volatility might be great for you or it might mean you should invest elsewhere. Either way, level II quotes will tell you.

Pivot Point Indicators

Pivot points are the levels at which price turns. If a stock is dropping but then makes an upward retracement, no matter how brief the retracement, the price at which it pivoted from downward motion to upward motion is a pivot point. This obviously holds true for stocks that pivot from upward to downward motions. These pivot points are useful because they indicate natural levels of support and resistance that the price is finding. Support and resistance are the barriers through which the price is hesitant to break. Some of these levels are due to psychological human quirks in the traders themselves. For instance, "round" numbers- those ending in 0 or 5- are more likely to be pivots than the rest. Numbers falling on the percentages laid out by Fibonacci are also natural pivot points. Other pivots come from the price action itself. Once a barrier has been breached, the point of the breach becomes a new level of support or resistance. This is most easily understood in an example. If a stock is trending downward, but historically it stays within a range, the point where it breaks the lower bound of that range is going to be a point that it will likely struggle to come back up through. So, if this stock does recover, when it is on its upswing, we can use that point to predict a pause in the price action. This might provide an attractive entry point. On the other hand, that same point may be too strong a resistance, and cause the stock price to turn again, back downward. That would suggest a new range with this point as part of the upper bound, rather than the lower bound it had been.

Bollinger band charts are a frequently-used method of predicting support and resistance. They are charted by plotting two lines, each two standard deviations away from the simple moving average. Because of the time delay and the amplifications of this charting method, the position of the average in relation to the bands indicated increasing or decreasing volatility. When the bands widen in distance from one another, volatility is increased, and vice versa. When the bands contract toward each other dramatically, this is known as a "squeeze" and it indicates that the market is likely to change direction soon. Bollinger bands, like other volatility indicators, should not be used on their own, but combine well with other methods.

Fibonacci Retracement Levels

Fibonacci levels are price levels that are calculated using the daily high and low for the security in question. As a scalper, you'll use the one day charts as well as 4 hour and hourly charts. Fibonacci was a mathematician who popularized the concept of the golden ratio. To chart Fibonacci levels, the distance between the high and low is divided by this ratio. These points form levels of subconscious support and resistance to traders. Roughly, they fall at 24%, 38%,

50%, 62% and 100% of the spread between the high and low of the day.

Fibonacci levels are similar to round numbers in that there is no real reason why support and resistance should settle around them, but it happens anyway. For whatever reason, traders are drawn to events at these levels, so respecting them is wise. They are particularly useful when looking for an entry point along a trend. Trendlines are not smooth, they are made up of growth, retracements, and consolidations along the line, These retracements and consolidations in particular are of interest to the day trader. They provide opportunities to enter or exit the market when it is still, allowing you to buy or sell at a point where the price has settled. On the short time frames you'll be examining, these are going to be very brief points. Their short longevity isn't an issue though. Since you'll have automated the orders you need to have executed, the periods of consolidation or infinitesimal retracements will serve to trigger those orders. It's more useful to think of them as guideposts rather than time-based opportunities. Scalping, more than possibly any other style of day trading, requires that you find these entries and exits easily and quickly. Since the sheer number of setups you're trying to identify is so large, having an easy way to plot entries and exits is invaluable.

Even though you will be using the daily, four hour, and hourly charts for most of your trade decisions, take a look at the longer-term charts as well. While the longer charts won't, obviously, provide the raw data that you need, comparing them to their short-term counterparts will train you to spot any discrepancies or historical price action data that may be important.

WHY SCALPING WORKS

Scalping combines the same decision-making methods used in swing and range trading, but condenses the time frame to very small intervals. Because the trade it so completed in such a short time frame, the risk is limited. An easy way to picture the risk mitigation scalping offers is to imagine a pool filled with hungry sharks. By quickly dipping your toe in and then jumping right back out, the sharks have less of an opportunity to gobble you up. Because the risk/reward ratio is so tight in scalping, you need to make a lot of trades. These trades should be diversified, like any smart portfolio. With both time limits and diversification limiting your risk, you simply need more of your trades to come out in your favor. This may seem obvious, but it bears spelling out. Other types of trading require you to gain much larger profits per winning trade, simply because the risks are so much greater. Good scalping strategies require you to set very tight stops, meaning that you'll never lose so much that your winning trades need to earn back all that much. When calculating what profits are necessary to absorb your losses, remember that your stop losses should always be set so that they are easily offset by the margin of your profit average above investment. This may cause you to miss out positions that look attractive, but remember that any position that you cannot afford to lose in is one you can't afford at all. Simply look for a better, more suitable trade that protects your risk-limiting strategies.

Calculating Risk

Setting a stop loss should be an integral part of setting up any position. It should happen automatically. Where you set your stop loss is dependant on how much profit you can expect to make on the trade, and vice versa. The take profit and stop loss orders work in tandem. The difference between the price at your entry point and the stop loss is the total risk of your trade. If your goal risk/reward ratio is 1:1, you'll set the take profit order at the same level above entry as your stop loss is below it.

For example, say you purchased 1 share Springs Inc for $60. You set the stop loss at $59.75. Your risk is $0.25. Therefore, you'll set your take profit order at $60.25.

Technically, any trade with a 1:1 risk/reward ratio is scalping. The term is only commonly used in intraday trades, though. Without the risk mitigation that the limited time spent in the market provides, this level of risk:reward isn't worth the trouble. The potential for profit only comes with a great many of these trades. Remember that there is no getting rid of risk. All you can do is mitigate what risk comes along with the strategies you're using.

Successful scalping relies on finding entries and exits quickly and taking action decisively. In order to do this, you'll need to examine the stocks, derivatives, or currencies very carefully. You can use the same criteria you would to rate an asset that you were planning to purchase and hold, simply on a smaller timeline. You'll need to be ready to monitor your trades as the transpire because even the best laid plans can go awry and you'll need to have your finger on the button should things need to be turned around.

SCALPING STOCKS

Speaking of strategies, the time has come to get into the nitty gritty details of how to choose, enter, and exit a scalping position. Hopefully by this point you have enough of an understanding of how scalping actually works that you are comfortable modifying these strategies to suit your particular investment needs. If you are working with a smaller amount of investment capital, for instance, you may need to raise the entry threshold so that you're only entering trades that meet a higher standard of certainty. This allows you to be more conservative while still engaging in the market. There are as many unique investment needs as there are traders, so feel free to tailor any of these strategies to yours.

5-8-13 SMA

The technical analysis of this strategy is very simple. Simply overlay the 5, 8, and 13 bar SMA charts and watch for a period where the 5 and 8 bar charts overlap. This 5-bar overlap is called a "ribbon." When all three bars overlap, this is a sign of consolidation that portends a reversal in trend or a breakout of a range. You may see the price action crossing the ribbon, sometimes in multiple places. When you see that pattern develop, watch closely. Soon afterward, you will likely see the ribbons flatten out and the lines begin to separate from one another. This is a perfect entry point on a short position. To calculate your entry here, look for the historical support levels for the price on the 12 and 26 day charts. Combine that information with any indicators you find in either Bollinger band charts or other pivot point indicators. You should set your stop (in this case, because this is a short position it would be a market buy order) at the first level of support because that is where your first trend-breaking risk is found. If the trend continues beyond that pivot, execute your next trade at that level, with the stop set at the same level below entry. Calculate your take profit orders (in this case they will be sell orders) by following your risk/reward ratio, whether it is 1:1, 1:1.25, or whatever other ratio suits your strategic needs.

Pair Trading

This strategy lends itself to being combined with a modified pair trading strategy. Since you are looking for points of divergence and consolidation between the simple moving average charts, you are primed to add in another set of the same charts. To day trade a pair, you'll need to find two assets that are strongly correlated. Exchange traded funds are wonderful for this, as it isn't difficult to find two funds that are based on the value of the same core asset. We'll use two funds that share the same underlying asset in the example that follows.

Traditional pair trading is done over the course of several days to a month. To make this strategy work in the context of day trading, you can simply use shorter term charts. In order to pair trade intraday, there needs to be a good amount of liquidity in both. Since both are based on the same underlying asset, they should have the same (or roughly the same) liquidity and therefore volatility. Overlay your SMA charts on both funds, and then wait for the ribbons made by the charts to diverge. When they've moved at least 5 or 6 ticks apart, enter the position by buying the lower priced of the two and selling short the higher priced one. The market will eventually correct the divergence and bring the two prices back together again, so your exits can be set at the next likely cross of the two price action lines. Because the two funds (or other products) have such a strong correlation, you can bet on them reconciling with each other, so your position is naturally hedged by holding the under- and over-performer.

While this is not strictly a scalping strategy, it can be treated very similarly. When two strongly correlated prices are experiencing a great amount of volatility, the resulting trend or swing can be broken up into many smaller trading opportunities. Pair trading becomes a scalping strategy when the risk/reward ratio is calculated to equal 1:1 or very near it and the trades are repeated several times through the day.

5-3-3 Stochastics

Stochastics are another type of chart used to measure volatility and momentum in markets. They are particularly valuable when you are trying to find an entry point in a stock or asset that is highly liquid. Widely-traded indices and stocks, in particular, can be very lucrative to scalpers, but it can be difficult to find reliable patterns in a very volatile market. This is where stochastics come in. These charts use different settings to control the amount of sensitivity to the market that they reflect. 5-3-3 is the most sensitive, meaning that it shows you the most true-to-market information. This is the setting you'll use anytime you use a stochastic chart. Scalpers need very precise, time-sensitive data simply because of how minute the trades can be.

To execute this trade, which is a long position, you'll need to watch for two things: an impending trend or breakout and a stochastic chart that crosses below the 20 line and then rises back above it. This is an indicator of the level of volatility that you need to anticipate the market movement. When you see these crosses, set your entry. You'll position your stops by looking at the Bollinger band charts. In this type of trade it is particularly helpful to use two sets of Bollinger bands. The first one can be the usual two standard deviations from the price action, but adding in a second one set at four standard deviations is helpful. This will give you multiple stops, which is useful in scalping because you're going to be finding several potential exit points. Once your first stop is set, your take profit level is easy; simply set it wherever it meets your risk/reward ratio.

4/12 Tick Pattern

This is a rule of thumb to finding entry and exit points for not just your initial trade along a trend, but for each trade that you make along the way. Once you've identified a breakout or trend, find your entry point by looking for levels of support and resistance. This method works for both long and short positions, but for simplicity's sake we'll just look at a long position taken on an uptrend. Your entry point in this type of trade will look like any other: it will be a short period of consolidation or even a retracement along the trend line. Once you enter, you'll set a take profit order 4 ticks above your entry. Your stop loss will, accordingly, be set 4 ticks below entry, giving you a 1:1 risk/reward ratio. If that trade tags the price and you exit with a profit, your next entry should be immediate (or close to it) but this time you will leave 12 ticks room for your stock to run. Your stop loss in this, and all of the following, trades will remain 4 points below entry. This changes your risk/reward ratio drastically, but for a reliable trend it's an acceptable change. You should exit the position entirely after the first trade that fails to tag that 12 tick gain.

All these strategies may all be modified in order to take into account your investment needs, but be careful not to change the values of any of the indicators. While time frame, thresholds, and relative indicator strengths are all quite variable, the fundamental ratios and levels are not. Many inexperienced traders run into problems when they fail to understand what parts of a strategy can be changed and which ones make up the core of why a particular tactic is effective. As always, keeping good records is the best antidote to this.

SCALPING FUTURES

Scalping futures is an exciting trading avenue with huge opportunity to make significant gains. Before we get into the best strategies to use when scalping futures, let's take a moment to refresh some of the particulars of futures that make them so valuable to a scalper.

First, futures are traded in "contracts," which means they are bundled into groups of 100 shares. This means the tick size is going to be significantly different than trading a single share. It's very common for tick size to be specified in the terms of the contract, so make sure you know what the size is before you decide to trade a futures contract. Just because a contract had a tick size of $12.50 last week doesn't mean that a different contract of the same stock will have the same tick size.

Secondly, futures are often traded in an index. This is an assortment of stocks on whose shares futures are issued that is then grouped together and the shared value of the futures contracts together are the asset being traded. The E mini S&P 500 is the most well-known and the largest of these, but there are others. Scalping these indices is an excellent strategy. When choosing an index to trade, make sure that it has enough volatility to meet your investment parameters. Some indices are much less liquid and therefore don't provide enough movement for scalping to be useful or profitable. Luckily, it's possible to evaluate performance of an index using the same momentum indicators that are effective with stocks.

Finally, futures trading is, by nature, more complex than trading in stocks. Because the terms of the contract add another layer of complexity to each transaction, you should be sure that you are appropriately set up to parse the level of information required. This means that futures should not be your first foray into trading, or day trading, or scalping in particular. Having a strong background in the stock market will hone your instincts and make you much more likely to succeed when you move into futures markets. It isn't just instincts that need to be developed. You'll also need to have a system for planning, executing, and recording your trades that you are comfortable with. The simpler the asset is that you start off with, there will be that much more room for error as you learn the strengths and weaknesses of your system and adjust it accordingly.

Don't let this turn you away from scalping futures. Just be aware of the additional levels of complication that it introduces to your trading day and react accordingly.

Scalping Indices

In these examples we will use the S&P 500 as the underlying index, but keep in mind that all of these strategies can be modified to be used on any index.

Pure Price Action

It is entirely possible to trade futures on price action alone. If your trades take place over a short enough time frame, the price action can provide all of the information you need to find, enter, and exit a position. You may use other indicators to confirm trends, but many traders make these decisions independently. To scalp on pure price action, you first need to find a strong trend or predictable range. Candlestick chart patterns are enough here, as long as the indicating patterns are strong ones. The key to making a pure price action trade work is staying in it for no more than three ticks in either direction. Even if the trend reverses, you won't be in the position long enough for too much damage to be done.

For instance, if you are looking to take up a short position on a downtrend, profiting off of the drop in price, the indicators of this down trend can be fairly subtle. Looking at 1-minute charts, wait for three candles to indicate the trend. At that point, borrow the futures contract (or contracts). Set the buy order that will close your position 3 ticks below your entry level. You should also have a "mental" stop and pull out of the position if the price does not drop on the second tick. When taking short positions, these mental stops are particularly important. The reason for this is that your potential risk is limitless in a short position, while the only profit you can make is the spread between the bid and the ask at the new price when you exit. Therefore, it pays to be quite risk-averse when trading short.

Trading the Volatility

In order to execute this type of trade, you'll need to find areas of greater or lesser volatility and set your stops accordingly. In order for that to exist, the asset being traded will need to be traded heavily enough to provide a good amount of liquidity. There are many indicators that track index volatility. For the S&P 500 this is the VIX. Bollinger bands are another ideal way to spot this volatility. Using a two standard deviation and four standard deviation Bollinger chart, look for periods where the bands are very distant from one another.

This signals increased volatility. Conversely, the bands coming together signals a drop in volatility.

Once you've determined the potential volatility in the index, you will set your take profits and stop losses accordingly. If volatility is high, set your take profit at 8 ticks above entry and your stop loss at 2 ticks below. This tight stop setting mitigates the risk of a highly volatile market. Obviously, the potential for profit is lower, but in some instances that's not a downside. This type of trading is especially valuable if you are trading an index that is strongly bounded in a range that moves about 10 ticks before pivoting.

In lower volatility markets, especially range bounded ones, setting up a wider spread between your take profit and stop loss is beneficial. When an index is bouncing up and down within a wide range, but doing so at a slow pace, its volatility is still relatively low. After confirming the low volatility with Bollinger band charts, enter the position at the low end of the range and set your stop loss 2 ticks below entry. Your take profit order, however, can be set as many as 30 ticks higher than your entry. This accounts for the low volatility by giving you more opportunity to gain from the trade. Raising your exit point naturally extends the amount of time you are likely to spend in a position.

This strategy is equally suitable to long and short positions. Simply reverse the take profit and stop loss orders in the above formulas.

Hedging

Hedging is way to balance the risk of your investment by making another, opposing investment. Futures and options are frequently used in this way as they offer a lower priced buy-in to the opposite movement that would increase value in the stock. Using scalping as a method of hedging can be a great way for a day trader to protect their other trades.

Here's an example of scalping as hedging in action:

Assume that generally your trading style is trend trading. You find intraday positions along the trends and set up your positions along the lines of the trends. You attempt to hold on to the asset for as long as the trend holds out in order to make as much profit as possible off of each trade. Now assume that the trade does not go in your favor. If you're not 100% certain that the trade will work out for you (and how could you be?), you could map out a scalping strategy that allows you to make some profit off of the trend moving in what would otherwise be the wrong direction. To do this, you would find the point at which you could safely identify that the trend is not going to break in the direction or at the velocity that you need it to. You would use the candle after the confirmation pattern as an entry point, and set your stops and take profits along the new trendline in accordance with market volatility. Then, you need only to execute the series of scalps along the trend to have significantly reduced, if not eliminated, the loss you took on the initial trade.

Or, say that you are making an investment based on a news event. If company XYZ is releasing a new product that has received a lot of buzz, it's fairly certain that, at least for a period of time, the price will go up. Since this isn't exactly insider knowledge, though, it's hard to make a profit based just on that information. What futures and scalping allow you to do is to enter the position and protect your investment from an improperly timed exit, which hopefully is what sets you apart from other traders hoping to make a buck of the same news event.

To execute this trade, enter the breakout as you normally would, scalping the duration of the price movement. Then, set short scalps on the futures contract of the same asset that trigger once the price moves within four or five bars of where you expect the breakout to exhaust itself. By doing this, you give yourself the ability to take profit from a wider range of trend-ending pivot points.

Of course, you can use futures to hedge in a more traditional sense. You can purchase futures outright to protect against scalps that aren't working out in your favor. By scalping an asset and then shorting a future on that asset, you're playing both sides, allowing you to realize a profit no matter which way it goes. This may be confusing at first, because it seems on the surface that simply not entering the position would be an easier solution to the problem of an unsure investment. But with futures, you can refuse to exercise the option if it won't be profitable. While it will cost you a little bit to purchase the contract, in this circumstance it acts as an insurance policy, and may very well be worth it to you.

SCALPING ON CURRENCY MARKETS

Foreign currency markets offer a unique opportunity for scalping. As we've seen, scalping is frequently totally reliant on the spread between the bid and the ask in order to be profitable. Since currencies are traded in pairs, the bid and the ask is evident within the pair itself. In order to explain this better, let's take a look at a forex pair and break down what each part of it means, and what they mean to a scalper, in particular.

EUR/USD=1.2501

In this example, the euro is the base currency. That means that it is the single unit of currency on which the value of the other currency is determined. Here, one euro is will buy 1.2501 United States dollars.

As you can see, the spread is very evident here. Additionally, since each currency pair purchase involves the "sale" of the other currency, the entries and exits are very clear and easy to read in forex. This aspect easily lends itself to scalping.

There are two considerations to be aware of before you look to do any trading in foreign currency. The first is that forex markets are highly liquid. There are simply fewer currency pairs than stocks to trade, so each one is traded more heavily. Beyond that, the majority of trades are made using only four pairs- the "majors," as they're known. Since every time a currency needs to be exchanged for another one, it happens on the forex market, the number of trades is huge. These factors come together to produce a much more liquid market than any other. This liquidity causes volatility to be comparatively very low. Given such a large pool, it takes a pretty seismic shift to cause a ripple. This leads us directly to the next important factor of forex trading.

Leverage is used much more widely and heavily in forex markets than in the stock market. Because the movements in the forex market tend to be very small, leverage is used to "amplify" them, giving them a weight and impact that would be very difficult for an individual investor to achieve alone. You'll need to be extremely familiar with the principles of leverage, your broker's policies on leverage and margin calls, and the amount of leverage you can cover should your investment go south.

Leverage Refresher

Leverage is the effect of margin, a loan given to you by your broker in order to allow you to make more or larger trades than you would be able to on your own. It's measured as a ratio between your investment and the investment made for you on behalf of your broker. If your broker approves you for a margin account, the securities and cash in your account become collateral for the margin. So, if you had leverage of 2:1, you would be able to buy $2,000 worth of securities while only using $1,000 of your own. If the trade tanked and you somehow lost the entire investment, you would be on the hook to your broker to pay back the $1,000 they had loaned you to make your leverage.

In stock markets, there are certain securities and derivatives that brokers don't allow to be purchased with leverage. This is because they are so volatile that the likelihood of the loan being repaid is too low for their risk threshold. In forex markets, volatility is extremely low so brokers are much more free with margin. It's not uncommon to find forex traders trading with leverage of 50:1, 100:1, or even 200:1. Because of this, each forex trade has another layer of complexity added to it above any other trade that is made without leverage.

Finally, margin carries with it one additional risk: a margin call. This is when your broker gets cold feet about an investment and pulls your loan. This can be disastrous if you are in the middle of a trade that you expect to see turn around, but the margin call comes before that ever materializes. Make sure that you're aware of your broker's policy on margin calls before you open your account. It's also worth taking a look into their past margin calls so that you're familiar with the circumstances that have led to margin being called in the past.

Scalping The Forex Spot Market

Scalping on forex markets is very similar to scalping on a futures market. The biggest difference is the amount of liquidity and how effectively it dampens volatility. There are steps to overcoming this. First, find a pair that's trending. It should be a fairly strong directional trend. In the upcoming examples, we'll use a pair that's trending upward.

Now you simply have to do what you would do if scalping any other trend: find the retracements and consolidations and plot your entries at those points. The chart pattern for these potential entries will likely be a rising range or ascending triangle. From these points you can also plot your pivot points. If the pair is trading in a range, you'll set your buy orders at the bottom points of the range and sell orders at the top, basically riding the retracements. In the case of a trend, you'll follow the trend all the way up, exiting when or just before it hits the level of resistance you don't think it can pierce.

Scalping a Forex Breakout

Trading a breakout is the easiest way to scalp on a forex market. Because the forex markets move so quickly and are so highly liquid, you need to be sure hard exits are determined before you enter the position. With stocks and futures you may find situations that benefit from manual execution of certain orders, but that won't apply to forex. First of all, with the amount of leverage involved, it is simply too risky. Secondly, the breakouts that we are looking to trade are very quick moving patterns and missing the exit by even a pip or two can eat into your overall profits by too large a margin.

In order to make this series of trades work, you'll need an idea of the historical price action in similar breakouts. You can get a very good idea of how much and how quickly a price is likely to rise if a breakout occurs by looking at the 28 day charts and noting the angle of ascent from previous breakouts. You'll use this angle to calculate your entry and exit points. Many trading programs offer this overlapping chart capability, but if yours doesn't, it's very easy to calculate by hand. However you do it, you'll need to find the likely breakout point using stochastics or another momentum indicator. Once that's done, look at your likely breakout angle based on the price action history. Then, along that line, find the levels of support and resistance. Those will likely be the pivot points for any retracement along the trend line.

Now that you have your trade entries and exits set, you need to figure out when to end the position altogether. This means finding a likely end to the breakout trend- a point where the price movement is exhausted and it will likely return to the previous level of momentum. The ideal situation is to exit your final scalp just before the trend you are scalping ends. While this is very hard to land on the nose, it's much easier to estimate the rough end of a trend and then find a stop level that will serve as a signal that the drop was not a simple retracement. Use your momentum indicators to find the general area where the reversal should occur, and then set your take profit order one or two pips *below* the anticipated high. Then, and this is key, *don't execute the order yet.* Manually exit once the peak has been reached and the drop has started. This is done in order to keep the automation from pulling you out before the peak. If you aren't comfortable exiting manually, you can set a conditional order that requires the price to hit a certain level before dropping to your take profit point before the order will be executed.

There is one market environment where this strategy is unnecessarily complicated and best avoided. When the breakout (or trend, or any other market movement) is unusually choppy, it becomes very difficult to ride through the retracements and know where the breakout it likely to end. Even though the choppiness provided more than enough volatility for scalping, if you are wiped out at the end of the overall trend because its end was impossible to predict, it does you little good. If you're trying to spot a breakout that can be scalped this way, look for historical breakouts with retracement lengths of no more than a pip. Any more muddies the waters too much to make solid trend predictions.

Automation increases the risk of exiting this position early, but setting your final exit for 2 or 3 pips (if the retracements only last 1 pip each) ensures that you don't get out of the position with lots of profit still left on the table.

Please don't fall for the snake oil salesmen on the internet who say that their program is a sure-fire and automatic way to predict the pivots that make up a range. The program that can do this effectively on its own simply hasn't been invented yet. If it had, everyone would use it! This is not to say you shouldn't use automation, just that the thresholds should be set by you so that the program is doing the best possible job reflecting your needs. You'll still need to be there to babysit your trades. Programs fail, markets turn on a dime, and there are a million things that could go wrong. You'll need to be there with your hand on the button.

Finally, some advice that applies to scalping generally but is even more important with forex trades: try to keep the size of your trades consistent. Not only is this important for monitoring your strategic success, it also prevents you from playing favorites. This is a trap that even smart, cold-blooded traders fall into. They put more eggs in the basket they feel is a little stronger, but then they favor that basket and leave their other, smaller baskets to their own devices. This is a terrible strategy! Scalping trades are all limited-potential trades. You need a pretty high number of them to come out in your favor if this strategy is going to be profitable for you.

CLOSING

We hope that you find the process of scalping both stocks and futures very rewarding. It's an exciting career path that many people have been wildly successful with. There are some common pitfalls, though, so we'll close this book by leaving you with our top three scalping tips:

- Don't let your emotions get the best of you. All of the hard work you put into your trading plan is there to protect you from becoming an emotional decision-maker halfway through a trade. Make sure your thresholds are set correctly and then simply trust them.

- As a scalper, most of your trades are going to need to come out in your favor in order for you to make a profit. This may seem obvious, but it isn't true with other trading disciplines! In some cases, the wins are large enough that they can easily make up for the more numerous, smaller losses. This isn't the case with scalping. Your profit potential is limited by the tight risk/reward ratio, so you'll need most of the trades to be winners. If they aren't reassess your trading strategy.

- Paper trade first! There are numerous virtual trading sites that allow you to practice your trades before you ever invest a single real dollar. Take advantage of this! The more you've used your broker's site, the better you'll be when you finally do go live. The more trades you've made virtually, the better your instincts will be.

We hope this helps in your day trading career, and that scalping proves to be a successful and profitable strategy for you. Happy trading!

www.ingramcontent.com/pod-product-compliance
Lightning Source LLC
Chambersburg PA
CBHW061222180526
45170CB00003B/1112